From GOOD to GREAT in New Home Sales

Myers Barnes

From Good to Great in New Home Sales
by Myers Barnes

Published by: MBA Publishing
P. O. Box 50
Kitty Hawk, N.C. 27949

Library of Congress Control Number: 2001 129186
ISBN: 0-9654858-7-0
Printed in the United States of America
0 9 8 7 6 5 4 3 2 1

TABLE OF CONTENTS

ACKNOWLEDGMENTS

My life is an incredible blessing. For that, I thank an almighty, loving God.

To my wife Lorena, my son Hunter and my Mom—you all are my reason to live and I adore you.

Ben Franklin once said, "Men can either buy their wisdom or they can borrow it from others." I'm surrounded by so many from whom I can borrow this wisdom, but will express my gratitude to three in particular. I'm indebted to my friend and editor Shirley Mozingo. You make me look good, and I appreciate you more than I can say. As we now produce our third book together, I extend a special thank you to Carolyn Porter and Alan Gadney at "One-On-One" book productions.

I am always mindful that no one goes it alone. So, finally, thanks to all my readers and customers who are eager to reach the top and have taken me along on the journey.

ABOUT THE AUTHOR

Consultant, motivator and author Myers Barnes is regarded as America's leading authority in New Home and New Community Sales, and is renowned for his management seminars and in-house sales training programs. In addition to his highly acclaimed book, *Reach The Top In New Home & Neighborhood Sales,* Myers is also the best-selling author of *Closing Strong, The Super Sales Handbook* and is the creator of the video/audio series *Follow-Up.* He is a featured columnist for *Professional Builder Magazine's* official website, Housingzone.com, and his articles regularly appear in many of the Nation's top trade publications.

Visit Myers at, www.myersbarnes.com
E-Mail Myers at sellmore@myersbarnes.com

INTRODUCTION

et me tell you a story—the ultimate story of *quest*
hope. You probably already know it because it
has appeared in every piece of literature you've
ever read.

It goes something like this. One day a
person—like you—decides to embark on a journey. It's a supernatural journey to do something
out of the ordinary ... something that will make a
difference in the world. Although your desire is to
accomplish great things and to be a hero, you're
unsure of your abilities and reluctant to leave the
comfort of your home.

But finally you do and are surprised to meet,
along the way, a very wise man who empowers you
with secrets, magic and words of wisdom. Feeling
more confident, you travel on, searching for a
castle in some faraway Camelot where you will do
wondrous things and find true happiness.

Armed with a pure heart and the wise man's
gifts, you assault the enemy, overcome challenges
and slay the persistent fire-breathing dragon. In the
end, you uncover a priceless treasure, win the
admiration of many and do live happily ever after.

The story sounds familiar, doesn't it? It's been the plot of fairy tales, movies, romance stories and even biographies.

That's because literature mimics life. We all hope for something better while struggling daily to overcome conflicts within ourselves and our world ... constantly seeking to slay those dragons of doubt, to discover a priceless treasure and to win accolades from a critical crowd. We dream of riding off into the sunset and living happily ever after.

But how many of us are willing to pay the price to make the dream the reality? Wouldn't it be simpler to fast-forward past the struggles and arrive at our just rewards?

Yes, it would be easier, but not better. Because it is the heat of battle that forges our spirit and fortifies our soul. It is the process of fighting dragons and overcoming obstacles that shapes each of us into who we are and makes us appreciate what we have.

Regardless of how you define success, this is evident: Success is NOT a matter of luck, an accident, coincidence and even a reward for a virtuous life. It evolves from a commitment to plan, prepare and persevere. Success does not come to you; you go to it. And although the trail is well marked, it is certainly not well worn.

Success is the result of making a conscious decision to backpack your emotional baggage, get up, step out and start over instead of sitting out life's game on the bench. To accomplish wondrous things and to reach Camelot, your vision must be followed by a venture. It is not enough to stare up the steps—you must also step up the stairs.

How do you do that? By realizing that you are the author of your own life story. If you don't like where you are today, do a rewrite. You can have a new life if you become a new person. That means reinventing yourself, refreshing old attitudes, discarding stale beliefs and reprogramming your thought patterns so you not only begin, but also anticipate a journey toward higher learning, self-improvement and personal success.

My vision is to impact the lives of others who are seeking a strategy ... a plan ... that will shatter their own self-limiting beliefs so they can become who they want to be and have what they want in life. That's why I write books, conduct seminars and do consulting.

My immediate goal is to impact your life—to be that "someone" Ralph Waldo Emerson referred to when he said, "What I need is someone who will make me do what I can."

As you read this book and we begin to travel the road to success together, I trust that it will lead you to sunsets, self-reliance and someplace where you'll live happily ever after. I pray that I will make a difference in your life. You have already made a difference in mine.

ICE CUBES TO ESKIMOS?

At a recent seminar, an attendee gave me a sincere compliment. She approached and stated, "Gosh, you are so good, you could sell ice cubes to Eskimos." Whenever I hear this, it causes me to reflect upon the awesome responsibility a person shoulders in the profession of New Home and Neighborhood Sales.

As a New Home/New Community Sales Professional, you are involved in what I consider to be the single most important profession in our country. You help people make one of the most significant decisions of their lives—specifically, how and where they will live their lives.

Regardless of whether you are selling a community of primary residences, second homes or retirement homes, you are helping people select the environment that will mold and shape their own lives and those of their families.

The challenge with selling ice to Eskimos or sand to a Sheik is, of course, that an Eskimo really doesn't need additional ice and the Sheik already has an abundance of sand. So, you're not selling as much as you're conning. You're in it for the sake of the deal; not the good of the customer.

Understand that professional selling skills are not tactics of the cunning used to manipulate people into purchasing what they cannot use, don't want, can't afford or don't need.

In the final analysis, professional selling isn't something you do to others, but rather something you do for them that improves their quality of life.

CHANGE IS NECESSARY—NOT NECESSARILY EASY

It's a paradox. Most of us admit that we want things to stay the same, but simultaneously get better. That is, of course, impossible. Nothing stays the same, including us. We are either improving or declining, going forward or backward, becoming freer or more addicted.

Change may be so incremental that you hardly notice any difference. Then one morning you awake and realize your body has suddenly aged, your attitude changed overnight or your interest level peaked or declined without warning.

Life is on the move, transported forward or backward by change and your reaction to it. You can't control all life's changes, but you can prevent them from controlling you.

Following is a poem that has had a dramatic impact in my life in being able to understand, cope and, more importantly, manage change. Perhaps you'll find it beneficial, too.

I am your constant companion.
I am your greatest helper or your heaviest burden.
I will push you onward or drag you down to failure.
I am completely at your command.
Half the things you do, you might as well turn over to me
And I will be able to do them quickly and correctly.
I am easily managed; you must merely be firm with me.
Show me exactly how you want something done,
And, after a few lessons, I will do it automatically.
I am the servant of all great men
And, alas, of all failures as well.
Those who are great, I have made great.
Those who are failures, I have made failures.
I am not a machine, though I work with all the
precision of one
That has the intelligence of a man.
You may run me for profit, or run me for ruin;
It makes no difference to me.
Take me, train me, be firm with me
And I will put the world at your feet.
Be easy with me, and I will destroy you.
Who am I?
I am Habit!

~ Author Unknown

Change can be good, especially when it breaks unproductive habits. Habits can be good, especially when they bring about necessary change. Use both to your benefit. It will help you keep mentally balanced. As Dr. Albert Einstein said, "To do the same thing over and over and expect a different result is the definition of insanity."

A final thought on change:

I live in an area where people earn a living by fishing and crabbing. When co-workers try to change professions or improve themselves, they want to avoid the "crab in a bucket syndrome."

When crabs are caught, they are usually placed in a container and piled on top of each other. If one crab tries to escape by climbing toward the top, the other crabs latch on with their claws and pull it down. People do the same thing, only their claws aren't as noticeable.

If you're trying to change, to break bad habits, to improve your job performance and your life, there will be those around you who try to pull you down. For whatever reason, they don't want you to escape the confines of your current existence. They want to keep you on their level. Don't let them. Even better: Avoid them.

To quote Mark Twain, "Keep away from people who try to belittle your ambitions. Small people always do that, but the really great make you feel that you too, can become great."

As a general rule, the most successful man in life is the man who has the best information

~ Benjamin Disraeli

MAKE GOOD ON
YOUR PROMISES

Most community salespeople believe we sell homes and homesites. This is only partly true. What we actually sell is a promise .... and wrapped around that promise is our sense of integrity.

Basically, what we say to our prospects during our sales presentations is, "You give me a check and I'll give you a promise to complete the transaction to your satisfaction. And with that promise comes my word that you will be receiving a new home of high quality, delivered on time, hassle free with no punch, completely warranted, and backed by my company." Pretty tall order, wouldn't you agree?

Since we're selling promises, we must be confident that what we promise can be delivered. Sometimes in the exuberance of the sales presentation (and during conversation), we make promises with the best of intentions; but something happens and we end up breaking them.

We may judge ourselves by our intentions, but our prospects and customers judge us by our actions. The proverb "Actions speak louder than words" is right on the mark. Your credibility in new home and neighborhood sales is established (or lost) on your ability to match promises with performance.

So, in the final analysis, it is best to under promise and over deliver. But in the event you can't deliver on a promise, accept complete responsibility and don't make excuses. Instead, be honest, fair and willing to do whatever it takes to compensate.

YOU GET WHAT YOU EXPECT— NOT WHAT YOU ALWAYS WANT

When conducting seminars, I share with my audience a true story about a man named Nick.

Nick was a strong, healthy railroad yardman who was consistently reliable on the job; however, he was also a devout pessimist who always seemed to fear the worse.

On one summer day the crews were let off early in recognition of a foreman's birthday. As the workmen left, Nick was accidentally locked in a refrigerator boxcar that was in for repairs.

He panicked. He banged with his fists until they were bloody and shouted until his voice went hoarse. Nick reasoned that the temperature in the car had to be near freezing and that, if he didn't get out, he would freeze to death. Shivering uncontrollably, he wrote a final message to his wife on a cardboard box that read: "So cold. Body's getting numb. If I could just go to sleep. These may be my last words."

The next day, the crew opened the boxcar doors and found Nick's body. An autopsy revealed that his body had all the signs of someone who froze to death. This was puzzling, however, because the car's refrigeration units were completely inoperable. The temperature inside was around 61 degrees and there was plenty of fresh air. What killed Nick was his perception of reality and his expectations that the worse would happen. And it did.

As tragic as the story is, it does illustrate that many people allow their fears to become self-fulfilling prophecies. In the Bible, Job is quoted, "The thing that I feared most, has come to pass." How true it is with many of us.

An acronym for FEAR is False Evidence Appearing Real. Nick believed the refrigerated boxcar was operating and that he would freeze to death. To him, this became reality. Fear clouded his judgment and immobilized him.

Everyone is afraid at one time or another. Yet, those who have the courage to face their fears will take action in spite of their doubts and uncertainty. You see, courage is not the lack of fear. Courage is the control and mastery of fear.

Actor Glenn Ford is quoted, "If you do not do the thing you fear, then the fear controls your life."

You develop courage when you force yourself to take action in the face of fear. So, go for that big sale. Try a different approach in marketing. Stop taking "no" for an answer. Stand up and try again. Remember, success is getting up one more time than you fall.

The bottom line? Recognize your fears, but don't resign yourself to them. As Emerson wrote, "Do the thing you fear and the death of fear is certain."

When a customer enters my store,
forget me. He or She is King or Queen.

~ John Wanamaker
He created the first department store and pioneered
the use of price tags, money-back guarantees,
newspaper ads and white sales.

REAL WORD OBJECTIONS ... REAL WORLD SOLUTIONS!

When the customer offers an objection to your sales presentation, is it really a rejection?

There are very few actual objections that are honest rejections. Most are just stalls from buyers hiding their true feelings. Why? Maybe they don't want to hurt your feelings or they are embarrassed or afraid to tell you the truth. Many times a pre-fabricated story (in their minds) is so much easier and less confrontational than actually telling the truth. So, they'll stall by saying something such as:

♦ I want to think about it.

♦ Do you have a brochure/business card?

- I have to talk this over with my wife, husband, children, parents, friend, brother, accountant, lawyer.
- I'll get back with you.
- I never purchase on impulse.

So, what is an honest objection? Frequently, they're not stated or addressed. But, most of the time when your prospect is stalling, his or her real objection probably lies within one or more of these categories:

- Location
- Competition (prospect has looked at other properties and is comparing)
- Performance/warranties (as to claims)
- Financing
- Needing third-party approval
- Price, square-foot pricing. (This is an objection of perception)

Once you can determine what the real objection is, and not the smoke screen, how can you confront it? Practice the Boy Scouts motto and Be Prepared.

In reality, there are no new objections. If you've been in sales for a while, you've heard them all before, in one way or another. The key is to know the objections that are most likely to occur, script the answers or responses ahead of time and memorize them so they become part of your regular presentation. Then, when you reach the close, you can respond to all their objections—both real and implied—with honesty and accuracy. Once you eliminate their objections, you'll also eliminate the feeling of rejection because you'll have honest reasons your prospects aren't buying. And, most likely, they have nothing to do with you personally.

In sales there is a universal axiom called The Law of Six, which states, "Customers really have no more than six objections to owning the home or homesite you're selling."

You may hear what seems like countless objections; however, if you categorize them, you will find they normally fall into six basic topics. Figure out what they are instead of waiting until you are involved in the presentation and then trying to make up an answer. You must be proactive and prepare in advance. Here's how the process works.

♦ Identify all possible objections—by yourself or brainstorm with team members.

- ◆ Write the objections down. Don't think it—ink it!
- ◆ Script potent responses. After identifying all objections, develop ironclad scripted responses and airtight answers.
- ◆ Rehearse the scripted responses in role-play. Practice, drill and rehearse, until your planned responses feel natural. This is professionalism of the highest degree.

Do this and, when the predictable objections surface, you can easily, effortlessly and automatically move to the close.

I am a great believer in luck, and I find the harder I work the more I have of it.

~ Thomas Jefferson

LESSONS FROM A
TIGHTROPE WALKER

In the 1800s there was a famous tightrope walker called Blondin (real name: Jean-Francois Gravlet) who earned his notoriety by crossing Niagara Falls on a tightrope many times, usually without the aid of a safety net.

Blondin's most ambitious and dangerous attempt was when he pushed a wheelbarrow loaded with a heavy sack of cement across the great chasm. With the extra weight, the slightest miscalculation could topple the wheelbarrow and plunge him 160 feet into the water below. Thousands watched in amazement as he made his way across—one foot in front of the other—oblivious to the danger.

When he touched ground on the opposite side, the crowd spontaneously cheered at the remarkable feat. Addressing them, Blondin challenged a nearby reporter by asking, "Do you believe I can do anything on a tightrope?"

The reporter replied, "Yes, Mr. Blondin, after what I have seen, I believe you can do anything on a tightrope."

Blondin further challenged, "Then, instead of a sack of cement, do you believe I could put a man in the wheelbarrow and, without a net, wheel him to the other side?"

"Yes sir, Mr. Blondin, I believe you can," replied the reporter. "Good!" said Blondin. "Then get in!"

Unwilling to take the risk, the reporter quietly faded into the crowd. It's one thing to believe, but another to have so much faith in a person that you put your life in his hands.

Yet, someone in the crowd did and the brave volunteer climbed into the wheelbarrow. This time, Blondin pushed his way back across the falls with a very nervous passenger. Wagers were flying and it looked as if Blondin would succeed. But, halfway across the 1,600-foot rope, a man with a heavy bet who was about to lose his wager, crept over and cut one of the guide wires. The tightrope pitched and Blondin fought to keep his balance. Realizing they could be seconds from death, he commanded his passenger to "stand up, stand up and grab my shoulders!"

Blondin's passenger was paralyzed. He again commanded, "Stand up! Let go of the wheel-barrow! Do it or we die!"

Somehow the passenger managed to stand up and Blondin shouted, "Put your arms around my neck and your legs around my waist." Amazingly, the man did as he was instructed. Clinging to Blondin, he watched the wheelbarrow tumble into the waterfall. Drawing on his experience, instincts and every trained muscle he had, Blondin inched his way across the remaining guide wire, carrying the volunteer and depositing him safely on the other side.

What's the lesson? There are two. First, whenever you attempt something above average, there are those who will—out of jealousy, anger, fear or ignorance—cut your guide wires. Shallow thinkers who are prisoners of their own comfort zones will slap you with criticism, ridicule you with laughter or heap on rejection. If you quit, they are also the first ones to say, "I told you so."

Consider these observations made by former doubters:

We don't like their sound. Groups with guitars are on the way out.

> ~ Decca executive in 1962,
> after rejecting the Beatles.

I'm just glad it'll be Clark Gable who's falling on his face and not Gary Cooper.

> ~ Gary Cooper after turning down
> the lead role in "Gone With The Wind"

Market research reports say America likes crispy cookies, not soft and chewy cookies like you make.

> ~ A store owner discouraging Debbi Fields'
> idea of selling Mrs. Fields' Cookies

We don't need you. You haven't gotten through college yet.

> ~ Hewlett Packard executive's reply to
> Steve Jobs, who founded Apple Computers.

The second lesson in the wheelbarrow story is that no one should go it alone in life. We need each other, and I personally am proud to shout from the rooftops that every one of my accomplishments has been blessed by having the valuable help of many unselfish and generous people.

So, whose help do you need?

The rule in obtaining cooperation is to be a go-giver, not a go-getter. Truly successful people are eager to help others. As motivator Zig Ziglar says, "You can have everything in life as long as you first help others get what they want"

The Bible refers to this as the principle of sowing and reaping. Socrates and Plato coined it "The Law of Cause and Effect." Regardless, if you help others, there will always be someone to help you to the other side. But, like the brave volunteer, you must do your part ... first.

Success is the child of hard work and perseverance. It cannot be coaxed or bribed. Pay the price and it is yours.

~ Orisom Sweet Marden

ADAPT A PH.D.
ATTITUDE

When I help my consulting clients recruit, hone and maintain a world-class sales team, I only recommend hiring Ph.Ds. Thinking I'm referring to an academic Ph.D., most do not initially understand that I'm suggesting they seek people who are Poor, Hungry and Driven.

I'm not talking about those who are literally poor and physically hungry. I'm talking about individuals who are lacking knowledge, but are constantly seeking to learn and gain wisdom. I'm referring to people who are hungry for success—who have that burning desire to accomplish and aren't satisfied with the status quo. Ordinary levels of achievement just aren't acceptable. These are people who are driven to set goals and to pursue them with bulldog tenacity.

Poor, Hungry and Driven people (Ph.Ds) have an old-fashioned work ethic. They expect to work hard … pay the price … and exert the extra effort. They go to bed grateful for the opportunities they have in life. Are you one of them?

You gain strength, courage and confidence by every experience in which you really stop to look fear in the face. The danger lies in refusing to face the fear, not in daring to come to grips with it. You must make yourself do the thing you think you cannot do...

~ Eleanor Roosevelt

LEADING ... NOT MANAGING

How did you rise to a management position in your company? If you're like me (and I'm speaking from experience), you advanced through the ranks by practicing superior sales performance. As a result, you became a manager without any formal management training. If this is true, then you may be failing your company twice. First, by being unprepared for the job and, second, by leaving a void when you advanced from the position of a superstar salesperson.

For a smooth transition from sales into management, apply these six principles.

1. Educate yourself prior to the promotion. In his management seminar, Tom Hopkins explained that, when he was asked to join management after an incredibly successful

streak as a salesperson, he said yes on one condition: He wanted six months of intensive, hands-on management education.

Unfortunately, many managers are promoted because of a crisis and receive their corporate baptism by fire. Regardless of how you attained your position, tabulate how many months, weeks, days or hours of formal management training (not practical experience) you have had. The answer is probably "not enough."

Management—like selling—is a skill. That's good news because, since it is a skill, it can be learned. So run to the bookstore or library and stock up on books written by those who have been there, done that and are willing to talk about it. Attend every seminar and management course you can. Search online for reputable material to get and free correspondence classes on management. Don't wait to be taught. Take a proactive approach. Become a scholarly sponge and you'll absorb success.

2. Recognize that you are no longer one of the "boys or girls." For new managers, this single aspect of crossing the line seems to present the greatest dilemma. One minute you are socializing with your friends around the water cooler and the next you are responsible for

their results. It is a casualty of the position that you must often forego friendship to establish leadership.

3. Stop managing and start leading. New home sales managers, beware! Don't buy into your title. No one wants a manager, but everyone wants a leader. It goes against our nature to feel like we're being "managed." It suggests that we're incapable of doing it on our own so we need supervision. But we all like role models who lead by example. What better way to learn?

    Leadership motivates—not manipulates—employees.

4. If you want to win the game, you better train before the event. Wayne Gretskey, the Mozart of hockey said, "I don't get paid for what I do on the ice, but for what I do between the times I'm on the ice."

    Beyond your own personal development, your team's education should include weekly training meeting (not policy sessions) to develop their skills. Bring in outside industry experts to enhance their education.

    I continue to be surprised when someone tells me, "Training is expensive. What if I spend money training them and they leave?" Here's a thought. What if you don't train them and they stay?

And here's one last tip. When you schedule a team training session or seminar that's conducted by others, plan on being present yourself. Your attendance and participation sends a clear message about your commitment to leadership and self-improvement.

Finally, and it bears repeating, continue training yourself. Attend every seminal possible, listen to sales and management tapes in your car every day and read a minimum of six books a year on management, sales and attitude.

5. Motivate and inspire. If you want success, you must create an atmosphere in which success can occur. In simplest terms, your job is reduced to two primary functions:

    ✓ A. Create profitable sales
    ✓ B. Extract extraordinary results from ordinary people

    Administrating, setting policy, dealing with reports and making sure the paperwork is accurate is effective management. Recognizing and rewarding great performance is good leadership. Getting out of the office and spending a minimum of 50% of your time coaching your sales staff is just plain smart.

6. Lead by example. The rule is simple: If occasionally you don't sell, you cannot coach others in sales. To stay in touch with reality, position yourself on the front lines. You need to know what brick walls your sales people encounter ... who your competitors are. Shadow your team members during their sales presentation. Observe how they meet and greet, qualify, demonstrate the site and close the sale.

Remember ...

If a team member loses focus, you have one person off track.
If a manager loses focus, you have the entire organization off track.

~ Myers Barnes

The potential of the average person is like a huge ocean unsailed, a new continent unexplored, a world of possibilities waiting to be released and channeled toward some great good.

~ Brian Tracy

BURN OUT OR
RUST OUT

Feeling burned out? Then consider this: To be burned out means that, at one point in your life, you must have been on fire.

If you are burned out now, then you must have been ignited to a temperature of almost white-hot excitement once. You were a roaring sphere of energy, enthusiasm and results. There was no stopping you.

What? You're thinking you were never quite that hot but you're still feeling burned out?

Then consider instead that maybe you're experiencing "rust out." The doctrine of entropy means that if you are not putting energy into something to make it better, then by default, it will become worse. If you don't use it, you lose it. This law applies to anything in the universe. If you don't exercise, you lose tone. If you don't feed your mind, your mental capacity and creativity diminish.

To see the physical results of entropy, look around you. If not maintained, paint peels, metal rusts, wood rots, cement crumbles and teeth decay. The same principle applies to relationships and to your business. If unattended they, too, will gradually deteriorate and you're left wondering what happened.

So, before acknowledging burn out, do an assessment and determine if, instead, you may be suffering from a severe case of rust out. Burn out is usually physical—you've pushed yourself too hard, too long. Rust out is most often psychological and the result of losing passion, energy and motivation. Your diagnosis will determine your new direction.

WANT TO MAKE
BETTER DECISIONS?

The people I respect most in business are generally instant decision-makers. Sure, if data is available, it is considered but they don't need to know every "minute" fact first. Confident decision-makers accept in advance that they are bound to make a fair share of wrong decisions, yet they are also confident in knowing that, most of the time, they will make the right decisions.

My friend and mentor Nido Qubien has a four-step decision-making method he shared with me that takes the risk out of decision-making.

Initially, he said, you must be willing to take a risk with your decisions, but as he emphasizes, "There is a difference between risk management and risk aversion."

Here's Nido's four-step formula to managing risk and making confident decisions:

1. Ask the question, "What is the best possible outcome that can occur if you were to move forward with your decision?" Then remove the rose-colored glasses, and ask the second question.

2. What is the most likely outcome that can occur if you decide to venture forward? In most cases, you will find the most likely outcome is the probable-case scenario. If the most likely outcome will move you toward your goal, then you are probably on the path to the right choice.

3. You have now pondered the best and the most likely outcomes, so step three is to ask, "What is the worst possible outcome of this decision?

4. Finally, ask yourself if the worst possible outcome should occur, are you willing to subject yourself and/or family to it?

After thinking through the outcomes, if you conclude that the most likely one will take you where you want to go but, if the worst outcome happens, you can live with it, then launch ahead confidently.

A final bit of advice—Most decisions are self-fulfilling prophecies. A lot of seemingly great decisions have worked; not because of the quality of the decisions, but rather because of the determination to make them work. Conversely, a lot of good decisions fail because the people who make them undermine their chances for success by not conquering their doubts.

Hiring Practices: How Long Does It Take You to Make a Decision?

Most executives decide whether or not a job candidate is suitable for the position in only four or five minutes, and then spend the rest of the interview looking for additional information to confirm their decisions. One study showed that 74 percent of the executives determine the suitability of the applicant within five minutes.

~ Printing Industries of
Northern California Newsletter

The greatest power that a person possesses is the power to choose.

~ J. Martin Kohe

The choice is yours. You hold the tiller. You can steer the course you choose in the direction of where you want to be — today, tomorrow, or in a distant time to come.

~W. Clement Stone

LET GO—YOUR OLD WAY OF SELLING WILL NOT WORK FOREVER

Remember bell-bottom jeans and leisure suits? We still wear clothes, just a different style. How about rotary phones? We still make calls, but with mobile phones.

Of course, there was a time a fax machine was high tech. But e-mail has replaced the paper trail. In shopping, Web sites represent storefronts and we can buy Aloha shirts in Hawaii without ever hearing a salesperson ask, "May I help you?"

We can now buy almost anything anywhere in the world and get everything from financing to furniture with the click of a button.

These changes in technology force us to make adjustments in the way we do business. Today, it's more important than ever to provide excellent service and to keep customer satisfaction high. You are competing internationally. To keep your sale's volume up, you must be able to sell the same customer three or four times. In other words, your customers must be so pleased with your service that they will buy from you again and recommend you to others.

✴ To achieve results from relationships, you must become adept at blending the old and new ways of selling—to take the old tried-and-true sales techniques and update them to suit today's new homebuyer. Memorize new sale's scripts. Practice other ways to meet and greet your clients. Learn how to reach a larger audience via the Internet. Develop a process that helps you attract more prospects. Find strategies and employ techniques that convince your prospect that you, your company and neighborhood/homes are the only choice.

How Can You Combine Old and New Selling Techniques?

For years you've carried a camera in your car to take pictures of homes so you can show them to prospects. With a scanner, you can transfer them into your computer and e-mail them to prospects.

Even better, upgrade to a digital camera so you can input photos directly into a computer for e-mail or printouts.

You should be mailing cards to clients on their birthdays, purchase-date anniversaries and holidays. In addition to this, e-mail them a monthly update about a community they expressed interest in, a style of home they liked, gardening or home repair tips, or new lifestyle products. Get current information online and then personalize it for your clients. This keeps your name in front of them regularly.

One absolute I have found is that the greatest salespeople of this age have the following qualities: an upbeat, positive attitude; a commitment to deliver the best service possible; current product knowledge; proven sale's techniques and strategies; and a desire to succeed that propels them toward their goals. There is one more thing. *Super Achievers practice selling.*

Within you right now is the power to do things you never dreamed possible. The power becomes available to you just as soon as you can change your beliefs.

~ Maxwell Maltz

LOOKIN' GOOD ...

Flash back to Carly Simon and her song "You're So Vain."

Now admit it: Didn't you think this part was about you?

A little dose of self-esteem is good. So, here are a few vain all-about-you practices to initiate that won't alienate others.

- ◆ Care for yourself
- ◆ Save for your retirement
- ◆ Work at being healthy
- ◆ Get trim
- ◆ Exercise regularly
- ◆ Eat with the following thought: Food is only fuel.
- ◆ Drive a clean car. It makes you feel better.

- Avoid heavy perfume and cologne. Others may be allergic.

- Wear quality clothes

- Think energetically

- Take vitamins

- Keep your shoes polished. It reflects favorably on you.

Is this vanity or self-esteem? You figure it out. I think salespeople who stand erect, look sharp and smile don't look vain ... they look like they value themselves.

FEED YOUR MIND

'll bet every time on the individuals who feed the best part of their natures (their minds) with the good, the clean, the powerful and the positive.

Why? Because they'll win over those who passively consume what the world dishes out. Rather than work on self-improvement, too many people vegetate in front of their electronics. Television, computers and video games are all worthwhile and entertaining, but they should never replace time set aside to think and grow. There must be a balance between entertainment and introspection.

Not only do many adults waste valuable, irreplaceable time sitting in front of a television, but they also set the example for the younger generation. Consider this: By the time the typical child has turned 18, he or she has watched more than 17,000 hours of television. This child has also listened to more than 11,000 hours of music and watched 2,000 hours of MTV and movies. This does not include socializing, talking on the telephone and dating. How much time in the 30,000 hours is actually aimed at self-development? Not much, if any.

Of course, the problem isn't only with the younger generation. A study focused on the typical American factory worker at a manufacturing plant. The person who worked by the hour on the line watched an average of 30 hours of television a week. The person in charge of the line viewed it an average of 25 hours per week. And the foreman of the manufacturing plant spent about 20 hours a week in front of the TV. (Are you noticing a trend?) The Plant Superintendent watched 12 to 15 hours of television a week, while the President of the manufacturing plant spent 8 to 12 hours watching television each week. Can you guess how much television the Chairman of the Board watched? His range was 4 to 8 hours a week.

Suppose the people who spend 30 hours a week in front of a TV reallocate just ten of those hours to their growth through personal development, self-help books, seminars and audio and video cassettes. Do you think they would have a career of working on the assembly line?

Part of your formula for success should be to feed yourself a steady diet of good information, which will not only help you earn a professional's income, but dramatically enhance your personal and family life.

As Jim Rohn, the business philosopher, said, "Work as hard on yourself as you do on your job," and I guarantee you will excel in the ever-changing profession of New Home & Neighborhood Sales.

It bears repeating: I'll bet every time on those who feed their minds with the good, the clean, the powerful and the positive.

A procrastinator puts off until tomorrow the things he has already put off until today.

~ John Maxwell

PROCRASTINATION

Rob Mason, a friend of mine who is an architect, made a profound yet simple observation recently. He said, "Imagine a health club where everyone who paid for memberships actually showed up to use them."

What's Rob's point? Many people want better lifestyles, but don't seriously do anything about it. One of the main reasons is that they put off taking action.

Procrastination is opportunity's assassin. It steals your time, creativity, motivation and potential. President John F. Kennedy observed, "There are risks and costs to a program of action, but they are far less than the long-range risk and cost of comfortable inaction."

As someone once told me, procrastination is the art of keeping up with yesterday.

Keep in mind that, while you procrastinate, life speeds by.

You are beaten to earth? Well, well, what's that? Come up with a smiling face. It's nothing against you to fall down flat; but to lie there, that's a disgrace.

~ Anonymous

FALLING FLAT ON YOUR BACK MAKES YOU LOOK UP!

I am constantly asked what I think the secret of success is. It's a lot of things, but these two points top my list:

1. Belief in yourself and your mission in life.

2. The ability to persist in the face of defeat.

When you study successful people you will see that they've made plenty of mistakes and have had countless learning experiences frequently disguised as failures. But they have one common trait: Whenever they were at the end of their ropes, they kept hanging on when others would have let go. Much like the Energizer bunny, they keep going and going and going.

For inspiration, here are some who didn't know how to quit.

♦ Dr. Seuss, whose first children's book was rejected by 23 publishers. If he had quit, the Grinch would never have been nominated for an Oscar this year.

♦ Albert Einstein had his Ph.D. dissertation rejected by The University of Bern because it was "irrelevant and fanciful."

♦ Noah Webster, who spent 36 years compiling Webster's Dictionary.

♦ Helen Keller, after losing her sight and hearing as a result of meningitis at age 19 months, became the first blind-deaf person to effectively communicate with the sighted and hearing world. Before age eight, she was an international celebrity. By the time she graduated from college magna cum laude, she was a highly intelligent, articulate and sensitive woman who labored incessantly for the betterment of others. Overcoming her "double dungeon of darkness," she wrote 14 books, traveled to 35 countries and met every president from Calvin Coolidge to John Kennedy. Winston Churchill called her "the greatest woman of our age."

♦ Johnny Unitas, rejected by the Pittsburgh Steelers and cut from the team, kept his dream alive by working construction and playing amateur ball until the Baltimore Colts finally picked him. He eventually became one of the most admired quarterbacks to ever play the game.

♦ Winston Churchill, a person who never quit in a lifetime of challenges and setbacks, may be best remembered for the shortest commencement address ever given. Speaking before the graduates of Oxford University he said, "Never give up!" A few seconds passed before he repeated, "Never, never give up!" Then, he returned to his seat.

Many things are lost for want of asking.

~ English proverb

THE ULTIMATE TRIAL CLOSE

What's a trial close? The purpose of a trial close is to evaluate and determine where you are with your prospect during your sale's conversation (presentation).

Unlike a close that concludes the home-buying decision, a trial close is used before asking for the final commitment. When using it, you are merely seeking the prospect's opinion and willingness to own. Actually asking for opinions (as in the trial close) is something you should perform regularly throughout your presentation. It's akin to checking your prospect's readiness-to-own pulse before completing the sale.

Here's the ultimate trial close. It should be asked 100 percent of the time before demonstrating your homes and/or property.

Superachiever: "Mr. and Mrs. Prospect, before looking at our homes/homesites, do you have any questions about the area, the neighborhood, our company and builders, or anything we may not have covered up to this point?"

Note: Remain silent and allow them to answer. You are looking for their feedback.

If the prospects answer "yes" to having questions, you can address their concerns during the remainder of your demonstration/presentation.

If the prospects say "no" to additional questions or concerns, you should be reassured that you will not receive objections about the area, neighborhood, company or builder at the conclusion of your presentation.

Keep in mind that the benefit of the trial close is to solicit feedback from your prospect. Because you are merely testing the waters, you don't end your presentation. Great salespeople use the trial close throughout the presentation to take the prospect's buying temperature.

LISTENING FOR
THE ANSWER

Telling is not selling. The professional salesperson knows this and questions skillfully
while listening attentively to the prospect's
needs. She asks her way into a sale. She doesn't try
to talk her way into it.

Was God telling us something when he gave
us two ears and one mouth? Perhaps the divine
message is that we should listen twice as much as
we talk.

Asking clients questions isn't enough. You
must listen to their responses. Then restate the
prospects' questions and answers to be sure you
understand. When you follow this procedure, you
not only discover how to assist your prospects in
their buying decisions but you also help them

analyze their own fuzzy thinking and confront their understanding (or lack of it) of relevant issues.

Six Ways to Improve Your Listening Skills:

1. Limit your own talking. You cannot listen and speak at the same time.

2. Listen actively by asking questions that give feedback. That means nodding and saying:

   - Let me be sure I understand. Are you saying that...?

   - Based on what you have told me, it seems the ideal home/homesite you are looking for is...?

   - Ms. Prospect, that makes perfect sense. Is what you are saying...?

3. Maintain eye contact. Be sure you look at the prospect as you ask and listen your way into the sale. It's frustrating to be talking with someone whose eyes constantly shift from side to side, or who looks away at something else in the room. Maintaining eye contact makes your prospects feel important and keeps them focused on the conversation.

4. Avoid interrupting. Sometimes a pause in the conversation doesn't mean your prospects have completed their thoughts.

5. Concentrate. Your prospect will know immediately if your mind is elsewhere.

6. Listen for feelings and not just ideas. Identify the emotional agenda the prospect is trying to convey. Take notes on key points and voice your concerns and observations.

Listening allows you to discover what your prospects need and to learn why they want a new home or homesite. Is it for profit? Relocation to a new school district? Social status? Pride of ownership? Do they want to move up in the world or scale down? What are their passions? If you actively listen, they will tell you exactly what is motivating them to buy.

Discipline is the ability to make yourself do what you need to do, when you should do it, whether you feel like it or not.

~ Elbert Hubbard

MANAGE TIME—
DON'T BANK IT

Have you ever said the words, "Someday, when I get time, I'm going to ..."

Regardless of our professions, most of us have an innate desire to become better organized, to get our lives and businesses under control and to find the time to do the things that are really important to us.

If I were to walk up to you and say, "Pardon me, what time is it?" how would you respond? You'd probably look at your watch and tell me, "It's two-forty-five (or something to that effect)." But how about this scenario? What if I were to ask you the same words, but in a rearranged order: "Time ... what is it?" How would you respond? What is your definition of time?

Defining Time

After pondering the question, Albert Einstein offered the simplest of definitions while introducing the idea of "simultaneous events." He said, "The train does not arrive at the station at 7:00 p.m. The train arrives at the station at the same moment the hand on the clock reaches seven p.m."

He was saying that time is actually how we measure events. Your reading this book is an event. Driving your car is an event. Answering e-mail is an event. Meeting with customers is an event. And each one takes up a certain amount of time.

Time management has nothing to do with the clock, but everything to do with organizing and controlling your participation in certain events that coordinate with the clock.

Einstein understood time management is an oxymoron. It cannot be managed. You can't save time, lose time, turn back the hands of time or have more time tomorrow than today. Time is unemotional, uncontrolled, unencumbered. It moves forward regardless of circumstances and, in the game of life, creates a level playing field for everyone. The paradox of time is that we rarely consider that we have enough of it when, in fact, all of it is available to everyone equally. You and

I—along with the rest of the world—start each and every day with the same 24-hours ... 1,440 minutes ... 86,400 seconds.

The only difference between being a productive person and a disorganized person is whether or not you grasp—either consciously or subconsciously—that you cannot manage time; you can only control the events within a given time frame. You can make use of time ... as in riding the train to the station ... but even if you choose to stay in the depot, the seconds will continue to click by on timeless tracks.

Perhaps the best known business example regarding time management occurred in the 1930's and involved management consultant Ivy Lee and Charles Schwab of Bethlehem Steel. Schwab challenged Lee saying, "Show me a way to get more things done and I'll pay you anything within reason."

Lee gave Schwab a blank sheet of paper and instructed him to "write down the most important tasks you have to do and then number them in order of importance. When you arrive in the morning, begin at number one (the most important) and stay with it until its completion. Once you've completed the most important task, begin number two and continue through the list all day long—only working on your most important task. If at the end of the day you have not completed your entire list, then don't worry. You couldn't have done so with any other method. Make this your habit every working day, and then send me a check for what you think its worth."

Weeks later, after Schwab found the prescription worthy, he sent Ivy Lee a check for $25,000, an incredible amount in the 1930's. When asked by his associates how he could justify such an enormous amount for such a simple idea, Schwab posed the question, "Aren't all good ideas basically simple?"

Schwab stated that the $25,000 was his most valuable investment and credited working off a list as the idea that turned Bethlehem Steel into the largest independent steel producer of that time.

To customize the concept, imagine that everybody in the world lives in rooms that are exactly the same size. There is no chance of enlarging their dimensions so the only thing differentiating us is the way in which we fill our rooms.

Some of us will buy lots of furniture and then get annoyed because we can hardly move around in the congestion. Others will buy less furniture but have it arranged in a disorderly fashion. These people complain about feeling cramped and unorganized.

Then there are those of us who invest in bookshelves, desks with lots of drawers, closets and organizers. We compartmentalize our belongings and, in doing so, make our lives less congested. Moving around, locating things and accomplishing goals is much easier.

Which room do you occupy?

THE THREE STEPS OF AN EFFECTIVE MANAGER OF EVENTS

STEP 1: Make a list of everything you have to accomplish under the topics of social, professional, civic, family, leisure, travel, consumption, solitude, creating, development, etc. You can only begin maximizing time when you know what you want to do with it. Once you are certain the list represents the events you would like to accomplish, move to Step 2.

STEP 2: Value each item on the list. How? By using the ABC method. As you go through your list a second time, put an "A" next to those tasks (events) that are "critical to be done." And then resolve, if nothing else gets done today, you will accomplish all the A's on your list. After valuing the A's, you then put a "B" by the events that are important to be done. However the caveat is, you will only work on the B's after you have fully completed your list of A's. You complete your list by writing a "C" next to any remaining items on your list. Your C's are relatively insignificant and are only worked on should you have discretionary time, after completing you're A's and B's.

Your goal is not to cram more things into an hour but to focus on the quality of those items on your list and how they fit within your overall goals.

STEP 3: Numerically sequence your events. You now review your list a third and final time, and revalue you're A's, B's and C's by their importance. Determine which A is the most important and then label it A1. The next most important would be A2. Then complete your list doing the same thing with your B's and C's.

I once heard Brain Tracy say, "Feeling listless? Make a list." Try this idea for 30 consecutive days and my personal guarantee is that your productively will increase by 20 to 30 percent. In fact, after one week of diligent application, I think you will not only experience astonishing satisfaction, but also absolute serenity.

(After you've applied the techniques, how about sharing your progress with me by e-mail at solutions@myersbarnes.com? I'd really appreciate knowing particular ways you benefitted that might help others.)

If a friend is in trouble, don't annoy him by asking if there is anything you can do. Think up something appropriate and do it.

~ Edgar Watson Howe

ENCOURAGING
OTHERS

Sales can be a dog-eat-dog, claw-your-way-to-the-top profession. But it doesn't have to be. Instead of a knife-in-the-back, how about delivering a pat-on-the-back?

The word "encourage" means to instill courage into others—saying something to others that causes them to like and feel good about themselves.

Everything you say that causes others to feel better about themselves causes you to feel better about yourself. Socrates deemed this universal law as Cause and Effect, and Jesus Christ pronounced this as the Law of Sowing and Reaping.

You are constructed by nature so that you cannot be uplifting to another person without being uplifted yourself. Conversely, you cannot tear down another person without tearing down yourself. Shakespeare wrote: "The fragrance of the rose lingers on the one who cast it." I might add, so does the fragrance of skunkweed. Be an encourager.

WHAT YOU SEE IS
WHAT YOU GET

I am regularly asked, "What questions do you ask prospective salespeople in an interview and what answers do you like to hear?

There are two basic questions I ask:

QUESTION 1: Would you describe the sales process as you know it? I expect for them to say, "Well, I have to meet, greet and qualify, then present and demonstrate, select one property, overcome objections, close or outline follow-up measures, then follow through to take care of the details until delivery, and finally obtain referrals." If they cannot explain the sales process, they won't be able to duplicate a sale consistently.

QUESTION 2: How much time do you spend on personal development and what books and tapes are in your personal development library? If an experienced salesperson doesn't have a personal development library, I encourage him or her to start one.

I also conclude interviews by asking sales-people how they respond when a customer says, "Well, I really need to think about it." If the person doesn't know how to respond to that— knowing it's the most common objection they will hear as a salesperson—then I know I have a lot of training to do. I also conduct a two- or three-step interview to see if candidates will follow up with me. If they don't follow up with me, they will not follow up with customers.

When I interview an inexperienced candidate, the main characteristic I look for is attitude. A new hire with a great attitude will naturally be positive and optimistic and possess a teachable spirit. After all, having a confident attitude is a key quality all top new home/new community sales professionals possess.

Keep in mind, when you are conducting an interview, that you are probably seeing that person at his or her best. They're going to look their best, behave their best, speak their best. If they are late for an interview, they will be late habitually, So, I look at their appearance and their entire demeanor, remembering that this is probably the best I'll see.

THE BEST PROSPECTS ARE YOUR PRESENT CUSTOMERS

Looking for new customers? Wondering where your next sale is coming from? Who isn't? You may not realize it, but you probably have countless prospects you are not paying attention to—namely, your present customers.

Consider the assets of a current, satisfied customer:

1. They know and trust you.

2. They are familiar with your company.

3. They live in a neighborhood and home you sold them.

4. They will return your phone calls and e-mail.

5. They will be receptive to your presentation.

6. They have proven their credit worthiness.

7. They have friends and relatives who may need a new home and their referrals are usually qualified buyers.

There are two methods you can use to increase your business in the profession of New Home and Neighborhood Sales. You can wait for company-generated walk-in traffic or you can proactively obtain more business from your existing customers.

Since every customer is a source of new business and referrals, the more profitable of the two options is to obtain new business from your existing customer base. Once you have satisfied a customer, that person will continue doing business with you if you follow up and stay in touch.

Here are some ideas to help you maintain and nurture the relationship:

1. Contact customers on holidays. Let them know you're thinking of them and want to wish them a happy holiday. If you've kept accurate notes on your customers, you can personalize your greeting by saying you're thinking of them because (a) he's a vet and it's Veterans Day; (b) she or he is a parent or grand-

parent and it's Mother's/Father's/Grand-parent's Day; (c) it's Thanksgiving and you're thankful that they've been your clients since 19—; it's Valentine's Day and you were recalling the story they told you about how they met or perhaps they are newlyweds and you sold them their first home; (d) you remembered their interest in cooking and you want to share a family bread recipe they might enjoy making during Easter; (e) you want to recommend a book you just finished that would be an ideal gift for their Aunt Elma or Uncle Ned at Christmas.

2. Contact customers by phone, mail or e-mail when there are new developments and changes in city ordinances, home-owner's associations, financing, insurance coverage, etc. If you are aware of a high appraisal that was recently completed on another house in their neighborhood, let them know. That may give them an incentive to sell their current home and buy another.

3. Stay in touch by sending them a personal newsletter. Keep it fairly short and diversified so it isn't simply a sales pitch. Include topics such as home activities to do with children, how to relocate elderly parents, hints for making your home sell quicker, what to look for in a remodeling contractor, how to

compare security systems and the latest home products on the market.

4. Call customers on the anniversary date of their purchase. Or send them an animated e-card.

5. Contact customers if there's a special event going on that you know they have an interest in. Example: A school fair, a craft festival, a fishing tournament, an antique show.

6. Many salespeople think that, unless they are calling customers to sell them something, it's a wasted call. It isn't. The call that's wasted is the one you don't make. So get busy and contact them!

You earn referrals and capture additional sales by excellent service. Remember, customer service is an act, while customer satisfaction is a commitment.

GETTING IN MEANS GETTING OUT

Lloyd Conant, one of the founders of Nightingale-Conant, the largest producer of audio programs on success in the world, came to the conclusion that "success is goals and all else is commentary." People with clearly written goals simply accomplish vastly more that those without them could ever imagine.

Let me ask you a question. If the evidence is conclusive, why is it then in every instance and every study only about three percent of adult Americans have a clearly written plan (goals) for their lives? I would suggest it's because, for most people, goals do not represent the opportunity to achieve, but rather the obligation to venture beyond one's comfort zone ... and nothing could be more accurate.

A goal is a planned conflict with your own status quo. In simplest terms, reaching a meaningful goal means doing something new and leaving the familiar terrain of your personal comfort zone. Probably one of the main reasons people do not set goals is because they must be willing to forsake old patterns and push toward new behaviors.

It has been said, "Fully 95 percent of everything you do is determined by your habits, good or bad." What is a habit? It is an automatic, trained response—a predictable ritual. Therefore, your first and greatest goal in life should be to form good habits that will automatically enhance the quality of your life, as well as broaden the scope of your achievements.

Remember, "Goal setting is a planned conflict with your own status quo." It's not what you necessarily need to do that keeps you from reaching what you want, but rather what you need to stop doing. In essence, goal setting is the realization that if you want a new result, you must be willing to become a new person. And that takes work.

As the saying goes, "Getting in means getting out." You cannot take on something new without consciously deciding to discontinue something old.

Effective goal setting requires the courage to stop doing the things that you know are destructive to your life and career. Like the early explorers, you, too, have new worlds to explore and conquer.

So what's stopping you?

Professional selling is 90% attitude, 50% technique, 80% persistence and 100% knowledge. The remaining percentage is luck.

~ Myers Barnes

FIVE COMMON SELLING ERRORS WITH AUTHENTIC SOLUTIONS

Error #1—Failure To Ask for the Sale. The main reason people do not buy is that they are not asked to own. Up to 50 percent of all sale's calls end without salespeople attempting to close … even once!

Solution—Memorize and internalize at least five closing techniques. The professional salesperson is like a professional actor and actress who has the scripts planted firmly in their subconscious minds. Master your closing dialogue (role-play and rehearse) before appearing on stage before your audience.

Error #2—The Deadly Sin: Prejudging. Prejudging is not prequalifying. Prejudging usually occurs during the initial moments of meeting a prospect. Many salespeople attempt to determine a customer's willingness and ability to own by his or her appearance, car or job.

Solution—Consider the advice of Henry Ward Beecher: When you want to know the worth of a man, count what is in him, not on him.

Error #3—Reluctance to Demonstrate Property and Homes. If the number one mistake with onsite sales is the failure to ask for the sale, then probably the second biggest mistake is failure to transition from the sale's center to the property and models.

Solution—You never ask permission to show potential clients your homes and homesites. Instead, you lead boldly and confidently. Top producers all say that going from the sales center to the property and models is merely a natural event. They simply say, "Let's go," and lead clients out the door. It's that easy!

Error #4—Apprehension to Qualify. As logical and sensible as it seems to qualify prospects, many salespeople still fail to do so. Spending time with qualified prospects is your key to a high sales volume. In fact, sale's research indicates that two-thirds of the presentations given by salespeople today is wasted on individuals who do not have the resources, desire, need to own or authority to purchase. Is it surprising that sales can be so frustrating?

Solution—Simply stated, you must guide them through the Process of Discovery and identify their wants, needs, desires, financial status and parameters, who the decision makers are, their time frame for buying, your competition and what objections might be forthcoming. For a more detailed answer and suggestions on how to implement the Process of Discovery, refer to Chapter 7, pages 71 through 92, in your copy of Reach The Top In New Home & Neighborhood Sales. If you do not have a personal copy and want to order one, visit our Web site www.myers barnes.com or call Lorena at 252-261-7611.

Error #5—Believing There is Nothing New to Learn. Like technology, professional selling today is evolving and changing more rapidly than in any other time in history. The seed of wisdom is the realization of how little we really know. Most people who excel in their professions are not impressed with how much knowledge they have, but how much they still have to learn.

Solution—A study by the University of Southern California confirms that, if you were to spend 60 minutes a day reading within your profession, then:

1. In three years you would be an authority.

2. In five years you would be an expert.

3. In seven years you would be in the top of your field and the best educated of your generation.

If you are saying to yourself, "I can't find an hour a day to read," then consider what you can accomplish by listening to audiocassettes in your automobile. If you are an average person, you spend 50 to 100 hours a month commuting to and from work in your car. If you were to spend that time listening to educational tapes instead of talking on your mobile phone or tuning into your favorite radio station, at the end of a year you would have significantly increased your knowledge and turned travel-time into teaching-time.

ALL THINGS COME
TO THOSE WHO
GO AFTER THEM

Will Rogers once said, "Even if you are on the right track, you'll get run over if you just sit there."

Information, knowledge and education are only useful when put into action. In our new economy, you can't just sit there and wait for your ship to come in. You have to be willing to jump in and swim out to it before the pier rots. As the saying goes, "It's better to wear out than to rust out."

Here's a scenario you might recognize.

There were once four people named Everybody, Somebody, Nobody and Anybody. An important job had to be done and Everybody

was sure Somebody would do it. Of course,
Anybody could have done it, but Nobody did it.
Therefore, Everybody blamed Somebody when
Nobody did what Anybody could have done.

Be a Somebody who is willing to make things happen. Follow the advice of Nike and "Just do it!"

SEVEN STRATEGIES THAT SELL THE CO-BROKER COMMUNITY ON SELLING WITH YOU

There are two existing paradigms (beliefs) that must be examined regarding sales that are co-brokered. First, understand that the developer and on-site sales teams often view the co-broker as being in their neighborhood, without knowledge of their homes or of how to work within a structured process. Second, the co-broker views the on-site sales team as an adversary, who is constantly trying to steal customers. This confrontational and nonproductive attitude on both sides must be changed.

Your True Customer is the Co-Broker

The astute community sales executive realizes that there are actually two buyers involved in the home/homesite decision-making process. There is the actual buyer and the co-broker who serves as the customer's assistant buyer. For the most part, the co-broker or assistant buyer has established a high level of trust with the customer and exerts a great deal of influence when it's time to make a decision to purchase.

Control is the key issue and understandably so. In the initial stages, co-brokers only want the on-site sales associate's brief overview and sales literature. What they do not want is for their customers to be taken over.

Therefore, on-site salespeople must acknowledge that the actual homebuyer is not the customer. The co-broker is. Consequently, 50 to 75 percent of the sale's conversation during the initial contact (meeting and greeting) and throughout the entire sale's process is directed to the co-broker. This is quite a revelation for some salespeople because it goes against their predetermined mindset.

Off-Site Co-Broke Marketing Strategies

1. **MLS is Leverage:** Join the Board of Realtors and become part of the team. A Realtor

operates under a code of ethics and deserves to work with like-minded individuals and companies.

2. **Handouts and Brochures:** The cooperating broker needs an abundance of off-site materials. Brochures, handouts and price sheets should be generic and should provide a space for the co-operating broker's card and personalized stamp.

3. **Clear Written Policy:** Have a policy and put it into writing. Make sure your on-site people are aware of the policy, as well as the co-brokers. It is imperative that brokers know their customers are protected when they visit your community.

4. **Communication:** Keep the lines of communication active through the process until the final closing. A good on-site sales executive is in touch, at the minimum, on a weekly basis with the buyer and with the co-broker.

5. **Give Closing Gifts:** Napoleon said, "I realize a strange secret ... men will die for ribbons." A bouquet of flowers delivered to the co-broker and buyer maintains the relationship and leaves a lasting impression.

6. **Pay Promptly:** Nothing stimulates and motivates a broker more that a fast payment.

Conversely, nothing demotivates faster than delayed compensation. This is an appropriate area to apply the Golden Rule.

7. **Contact the Broker-In-Charge:** Send a letter to the cooperating broker congratulating him or her on setting a fine example and on being easy to work with. Acknowledge that you look forward to your next association with him or her.

DRESS TO SELL

In the eighties, John T. Molloy's book "Dress for Success" directed the sales professional to wear a (dark) blue suit, blue or white shirt and red power-tie. Women were told to don below-the-knee skirts, jackets and, of course, no ostentatious jewelry.

Today, it seems we have evolved into very casual attire. Should we as professionals have a problem with that? I think the answer is "yes."

In my travels, I am noticing that sales professionals are pushing the envelope and going beyond casual into "at-home wear." I have to wonder what their customers think when their sales representatives show up wearing wrinkled khakis, short-shorts, collar-less shirts, sandals and sometimes even provocative clothing.

Understand I'm not a prude. I just believe that the way we package ourselves makes a statement about what we think of ourselves. Experts agree that judgment is being passed in the first one to four seconds that a prospect and salesperson meet and the judgment is finalized and completed within the first 30-seconds. If your prospect's first glance is favorable, you may expect him to act and respond positively during your sales conversation. However, if your prospect's first impression is negative, you're already at a disadvantage. Your prospect might wonder: Does your sloppy appearance translate into carelessness in business? Is your too-casual dress code an indication that you don't take your job seriously? If you don't pay attention to your appearance, are you also negligent in details?

Adhere to this adage throughout your selling career: "First impressions are lasting impressions and you will never get a second chance to make a good first impression."

Excellent grooming and appropriate clothing set the first and lasting impression your prospects and customers form. They speak volumes about you and your company.

As an effective salesperson or manager, you want your clothes to not only command respect but also position you as an authority on the neighborhood and homes you represent.

The following books are assets in helping you refine your personal image.

1. *Dress For Success.* John T. Malloy, version for both women and men.

2. *Casual Power: How to Power Up Your Non Verbal Communication and Dress Down for Success:* Sherry Maysonave, Bright Books, Inc.

It's so hard when I have to, and so easy when I want to.

~ Sandra Anice Barnes

TRUST IS
EVERYTHING

In the mid-eighties, companies spent 80 to 90 percent of their sale's training efforts on product knowledge, with only 10 to 20 percent of their effort focused on selling and developing psychological skills. In essence, the successful salesperson of the past was trained to be a walking product encyclopedia—nothing more than a talking brochure.

Today, customers have easy access to product information and can quickly find data, competitive comparisons and pricing on the Internet. The salesperson who dispenses product information like a vending machine will have a difficult time competing in our ever-changing new economy.

Factors important in today's sales environment are:

- ◆ Business acumen
- ◆ Trust
- ◆ Intra-personal skills

The trust bond between the salesperson and prospect is the foundation of today's selling environment. Trust is everything. And it is strengthened by the simple act of listening.

You build high levels of trust by asking questions aimed at determining the real needs, wants and desires of your customers ... and by listening to their replies. This give-and-take deepens your and your customers' grasp of what is truly significant in their situations. When trust is high enough, the sale will occur.

Since you have two ears and one mouth, use them proportionately. Listen as if nothing else is more important than the words of your customer and you will have more sales than you can imagine. People gravitate to the salesperson who listens thoughtfully to their circumstances and, after listening, offers advice they can trust.

CONQUERING FEAR

Fear percolates through your thinking and
makes you the landlord of a terrible tenant. It's
like a virus, permeating your body, breeding in
your mind, eating away your spirit. But fear can be
the first step to something better. With a little more
courage and a little more faith, you can have
victory.

Ralph Waldo Emerson said that one day he
was walking down the streets of Concord,
Massachusetts, and a piece of paper blew against
his leg that forever changed his life. It read: If you
would choose to be happy and successful, make a
habit throughout your life of doing the things you
fear.

Why do people fail in selling? Fear of rejection.
So what do most of them do? They avoid their
fears and, by not confronting their areas of
concern, it makes them even more fearful and
anxious. One-third of all salespeople drop out

because they cannot take the fear and trauma of rejection. Conversely, the top salespeople do it differently by continually confronting their fears.

Aristotle coined the word PRACTICE. In its Greek text it means "taking action consistent to the desired outcome." If you want to develop a skill—even courage—engage in the action repeatedly until you develop the habit. In Aristotle's own words, "If you desire a quality and you have it not, act in every respect as if you already possess the quality you desire and you will have it."

THE "QUICK-FIX"
MENTALITY

We all have a quick-fix mentality. When facing challenges, we look for instant solutions.

We tend to search for the quick book, quick tape, quick seminar, looking for that one idea that will solve all our problems.

Suppose you were 30 pounds overweight and I said to you, "I have a technique that will help you lose that weight in one minute or one hour." Would you believe me? The truth is you'd probably be a little skeptical and yet we hear stuff like this all the time from those who are selling "snake oil." Don't get suckered in. How long did it take you to get to where you are at this point in your life? Years? Then don't expect overnight changes. It's going to take time to get you to where you want to go. There's no quick fix, no shortcut, on the real road to success. You develop by doing and progress by practicing.

People come to me in training seminars and say, "I want to become excellent in selling. What's the one book, one tape, one thing I need to know to become really good?" My reply is always the same—The one thing you need to know is to give yourself one year.

Start a one-year personal growth and development project. Set a goal, develop a plan and get a series of books and tapes on selling. Above all, avoid the temptation of trying to become the best too quickly. Why? Because, just like a dieter who climbs on the scales daily, if you don't see the results quickly , you will become discouraged. The only thing you should do quickly is to start immediately, avoid procrastination and then give yourself time. There is a season for everything—even success.

As a general rule, reading a book a month will work, while simultaneously committing to a tape series. Then, go out every day and practice what you learn. At the end of a year (not a day, week or month), evaluate your progress. You will be amazed at how far you have progressed, and shouldn't be surprised if you've tripled your sales.

Be patient and persistent. Don't try to change yourself in an instant. Henry Ford said, "The keys to success are patience and foresight. The man or woman who lacks this is not cut out for business."

Make every thought, every fact, that comes into your mind pay you a profit. Make it work and produce for you. Think of things not as they are but as they might be ... don't merely dream — but create!

~ Robert Collier

CLOSING THE SALE:
THE FORGOTTEN ART

There are strategies to follow in closing a sale successfully. Yet some sales-training professionals and salespeople say that to learn specific closing techniques is to revert to an obsolete era of the sales profession. It has even been suggested that closing techniques are nothing more than customer manipulation.

This simply is not true. There are many components to closing a sale and not all of them occur at the time of the sale. For example, if you create a fabulous presentation with a good script designed only to close the sale, you are not seeking a relationship with the customer but merely a one-night stand because you are neglecting the importance of follow up. Then, you might manipulate the customer into making the decision that you want rather than the one that would best satisfy his or her needs. You may get them once, but will they give you referrals or call you again?

Some sales trainers believe that success in selling is a number's game. If you make enough calls, a percentage of sales will almost occur by themselves. And they will. But think of all those sales you didn't make that you could have if you had closed strategically to a process.

Granted, we are closing sales differently today than in the seventies, eighties and nineties, but there are fundamentals that have always worked and will continue to work, culminating in great success in a salesperson's career.

Relationship selling, partnering and consultive selling are valid, modern-day selling strategies. However, they certainly are not meant to supplant the time-honored skill of closing but rather to supplement it.

Some buying situations call for salespeople to operate on the premise of the one-time call and close. Others may require spending months or even years working with prospects to determine needs and build trust and credibility before closing the transaction. Regardless, it still comes down to gaining commitment and reaching the final agreement, which is closing the sale.

There are, in my estimation, these six basic critical steps to a sale:

1. Meet and greet
2. Discovery/qualification
3. Presentation/demonstration
4. Handling objections
5. Closing the sale
6. Following up and following through

If you carefully analyze the six steps, you will notice that every one requires specific closing techniques and skills. As each step is completed, the sale moves toward the end result.

When Vince Lombardi assumed the position of head coach for the Green Bay Packers, he was asked his strategy to turn around and lead the struggling team to its eventual number-one position. Mr. Lombardi replied, "I plan to lead by becoming brilliant at the basics." The basics for him were passing, running and kicking the ball. Regardless of criticism from skeptics, Lombardi never lost his focus. He coached Green Bay to five NFL titles, won two Super Bowls and died as NFL's all-time winningest coach with a .740 percentage.

The basics for you as a professional sales-person are the six critical steps to selling. Like Lombardi, if you become brilliant at the basics—including closing—you, too, can reach the top.

You may spend a lot of time with a prospect, but in the end, if you do not close, you do not get paid. Closing is not an event that will occur on its own. Even if you have a phenomenal relationship with a prospect and you deliver an excellent presentation, you must be prepared to ask for the order.

You cannot delude yourself into believing that the presentation, numerous sales calls and a solid relationship are all that's necessary to entice a prospect to buy. There must be that one final step that only you can initiate and complete. In any sale's transaction, there must be closure before there's a check.

COACHING YOUR SALE'S TEAM

If a super achiever like Tiger Woods or a company like General Electric can have one or more personal coaches guiding their development, wouldn't your sale's team benefit by having one, too?

The success of your company will be based upon many things, but one of the primary components is "the sales manager."

A sales manager can make or break a company by motivating or malingering ... by exhibiting an attitude that's inspiring or indifferent toward the sale's staff. Today's leaders recognize the importance of educating the sale's team, but further acknowledge the necessity of coaching one-on-one with individual team members on a consistent basis.

It is estimated that the average salesperson works at less than 50 percent of his or her capacity. Coaching breaks that cycle and allows the salesperson to live by design, not by default. It provides guidance and encouragement by helping individuals go where they could not go by themselves. It maps the road ahead so they are not wandering aimlessly, being deterred by imaginary roadblocks and taking procrastination detours. The salesperson becomes accountable not only to their coach, but also to individual and company goals.

To Be an Effective Coach, Here Are Five Steps to Follow.

Step 1: Shadowing

Coaching involves your determination that each individual salesperson must have a complete understanding of the sale's process. Therefore, you must observe each team member's selling process and the skills of that person in action.

This means that first you must commit to management by observation. Get out in the field with your foot soldiers. Free yourself of your desk, mobile phone, meetings, computer, and all the activities that keep you managing instead of coaching.

Secondly, when observing the sale's process between salesperson and prospect, you must resolve to not become involved in the conversation. It's vital that the team member understands in advance that you will not step in and take over any part of the selling procedure. The purpose of shadowing is to make observations that can give you insight into what works and what areas need improvement. So remember, in the field, you're shadowing ... not sharing.

Step 2: Get The Salesperson's Feedback

The art of effective coaching is to first get, not give, feedback. Your role is to ask questions so that the salesperson can sit back and analyze what happened during the sale's process. If you can help your students analyze their actions and form their own conclusions, they will be more willing to accept that a change in their approach might be in order.

Here are questions that elicit feedback and help the salesperson:

♦ **What was the objective of your sale's presentation?** (As a coach, you must have them keeping "the end in mind," which is to "bring about a sale." If this is not the primary objective, the salesperson is merely having a social visit with company-generated prospects.)

♦ **What did you do right?** (Find positives and reinforce them through the coaching process.)

♦ **What could you have done differently?** (Avoid saying, "What did you do wrong?" That can be unintentional destructive criticism.)

♦ Based on the outcome of that call, **what one area of the sale's process do you think you could strengthen** that would improve your results? (Review the process: **Meet & Greet. Present/overview. Demonstrate. Objections/Close.** Whatever part they identify as their stumbling block, work with them immediately to establish a plan for improvement.)

As the salesperson answers these questions, reinforce their answers with the most powerful one-word question you can ask to cause them to elaborate. And that is, "Why?" Why is that part of the selling strategy? Why do you believe or disbelieve a particular technique and strategy will or will not work? Why do you think the prospect reacted the way he did? Why do you think you need to strengthen a particular area of your sale's process?

Step 3: Demonstrate the Solutions

It is important that the salesperson witnesses the skills that they are attempting to learn being demonstrated by someone else. In demonstrating desired behaviors and outcomes, the coach should (1) establish objectives for all sale's calls (2) role play with the salesperson using the proper scripts and dialogue (3) be willing to reverse the roles and sell a prospect with the salesperson observing and (4) give a detailed action plan, the reason behind it, and follow-up

Step 4: Reinforce

Because people change slowly and for their own reasons, coaching is a process. Performing steps one through three will not result in new productive habits being developed overnight. Repetition is the mother of learning and only reinforcing the behaviors regularly will create lasting results. So be patient and persistent.

Step 5: The Final Analysis

You cannot teach something you have not learned and mastered yourself. I'm certain you have heard the adage, "Practice makes perfect." Well, nothing could be further from the truth. Practice does not make perfect; it only makes permanent. As the great golfer Lee Trevino said, "Practice a good swing or a bad swing long enough and it becomes a habit." In other words, only perfect practice makes perfect.

As a coach, you're accountable to your salespeople. *When you can show your team, you show them that you know it. When you can't show your team, you show them that you don't know it. And they will be watching.*

MOTIVATING YOUR PEOPLE FOR PEAK PERFORMANCE

The greatest untapped resource in any organization—and its most expensive—is its work force. It has been estimated that the average person at any given time works less than 50 percent of his or her capacity. If this is true—and I believe it is—then a good manager can increase productivity without increasing payroll by helping his or her people work more efficiently.

As I see it, there are two key functions of an effective manager. One is to help the company make a profit. And the second is to motivate the sales team to achieve their full potential.

Of course, as a sales manager, the better your team performs, the healthier your bottom line. So, in essence, the results you want are always held in escrow by those you supervise. Obviously, it's to your benefit to motivate your sales team to achieve extraordinary sales. How do you do that?

Conventional wisdom dictates that money and benefits are all that is necessary to attract and maintain a world-class sales organization. But the truth is that, beyond a certain point, money and benefits are only important in keeping people satisfied. They do not play an exclusive role in motivating them beyond average levels. What does?

The Three R's of Motivation: Recognition Rewards and Reinforcement.

Recognition: People crave recognition. They want others to know who they are and what they are achieving. By focusing on and rewarding positive behaviors—by showing appreciation and placing attention on the good things people do— you actually reinforce their desire to continuously do the right thing. The double win is that recognition also helps build a positive self-image, which further develops a positive attitude.

Unfortunately, in many organizations, autocratic leaders tend to criticize, condemn and complain ... never forgetting a negative performance while good performances go unnoticed. They harp on mistakes, unaware that by default they are re-enforcing undesirable behaviors.

The famous psychologist, B.F. Skinner was noted for saying that since we are all attention-seeking organisms, we will continue negative behavior because it gets us the desired result. Being criticized is a way of receiving attention; some people prefer that to no recognition at all.

Instead of pointing out what is wrong in a person's behavior, focus on what is good. Make a habit of celebrating the achievements (large and small) of individuals and teams.

Lee Iaccoca said many years ago, "When I reprimand, it is always orally and in private; when I praise someone, it is always in writing as well as in public."

So, never hesitate to let your entire staff in on the praise. If other team members are aware of the recognition, it may spur them to work toward similar achievements.

Rewards: Napoleon observed, "Men will die for ribbons." Telling people you appreciate them is a good beginning, but etching it in stone is even better. A personal thank-you card that recognizes in detail a special accomplishment gives the recipient a form of praise that endures and can be shown to co-workers, friends and family. In addition, something to hang on the wall—a certificate or plaque—is a permanent reminder.

No matter what type of reward you give for extraordinary performance—cash, gift certificates, tickets to an event, a trip to a resort—spending a few extra dollars for a certificate or plaque is a monument to the person and a constant reminder of your appreciation.

Reinforcement: Singling out an associate every month to praise is probably the most popular form of individual recognition ... as with the salesperson or employee of the month program.

But any form of reward can be effective—some for short periods and others for much longer. Regardless of how you recognize achievement, you must consciously reinforce the behaviors associated with peak performance.

A final thought. In rewarding salespeople, keep in mind that actual results, not politics, should be the sole basis for all recognition. Rewards should only be given to those who have sincerely earned them. Otherwise, your incentive program will backfire and foster resentment.

Using the Best Motivator of All

Motivation is more than a well-thought-out reward program. To really stimulate your team, a climate of self-motivation needs to be created that promotes growth and personal development.

The best way to motivate your team is to build their self-confidence. Realize a salesperson's self-confidence is on the line every time he or she encounters a potential homebuyer. That's why the single best motivator is to provide salespeople with the skills needed to excel in their profession. People naturally enjoy doing that which they do well and fueling their level of competence will increase their self-confidence and decrease their fear of rejection.

Continuous training and education are necessary to keep a company thriving. Many organizations report up to a 30-to-one payoff in improved performance from consistent training. However, it is estimated that the average company spends up to 85 percent of its operating cost on payroll and less than one percent on developing the skills of their work force.

A predictable objection concerning staff education is the "myth of the expense." Expense is perceived as cost, and cost is associated with no return. An investment, on the other hand, is when a tangible return is realized. Therefore, education and training should be perceived as an investment that will yield a return rather than a cost that depletes revenue.

The highest compliment an organization can pay its people and the greatest message it can send to the entire staff is, "We believe in your potential; our future and yours is long-term. Therefore, we are investing in your personal development, which insures our company's growth and yours."

Everyone has inside him a piece of good news. The good news is that you don't know how great you can be! How much you can love! What you accomplish! And what your potential is!

~ Anne Frank

PROFILE YOUR PEOPLE

There is an age-old parable that demonstrates the benefit of profiling potential new team members during the selection process. It goes like this:

> There once lived a scorpion and a frog, *who by nature* were natural enemies.
>
> One day, out of necessity, the scorpion had to cross a pond, but being a scorpion he couldn't swim. So he approached the frog and asked, "Please, Mr. Frog, won't you consider carrying me across the pond on your back?"
>
> "You can't be serious." replied the frog. "Why would I consider placing myself in danger, knowing you will sting me as I swim across?"

The scorpion replied, "But why would I sting you? It's not in my best interest to sting you, because if I sting you, then I will drown."

Although the frog knew the *nature* of the scorpion and how lethal he was, the logic of the argument made perfect sense. Wanting to believe the best, the frog felt in this one instance the scorpion would keep his tail in check. So, the frog reluctantly agreed. The scorpion climbed aboard the frog's back and they set off across the pond. Just as the frog reached the embankment on the other side, the scorpion set his tail and stung the frog. Mortally wounded, the frog cried out his last words: "How could you sting me? You promised!"

"I know," replied the scorpion, as he walked away from the frog. "But after all, I am a scorpion. I have to sting you. It's my *nature*."

If you doubt the validity of administering a personality profile on all prospective employees, remember what the frog forgot: Past behavior will normally predict future conduct.

Because individuals are so complex (yourself included), even the best hiring skills will give you only a certain insight and success rate. Each person is motivated differently and, because we are individuals, we have our own way of thinking and relating to others. Sometimes we adjust to others readily; other times we antagonize them.

Simple as it may seem, this is a difficult insight for many to accept. But the reality is, whether you profile job candidates or not, you will eventually learn their true nature. So, it's better to find out as much as you can beforehand. Otherwise, you might discover that experience is defined as "knowing what you shouldn't have done, if you had it to do all over again."

Today's preparation equals tomorrow's performance.

~ David Duval
Professional Golfer

FAILING FORWARD

Every profession in the world has its own failure rate. Yet sales is the only profession where the standard, normal rate of failure can be as high as 80 to 90 percent.

In my estimation, the difference between failure and success is perception. Your perception will always be your reality. Therefore, do not perceive FAILURE as anything other than a necessary learning experience that must occur to achieve success. George Bernard Shaw put it this way: "When I was young, I observed that nine out of ten things I did were failures. So I did ten times more work."

Consider the failures in the life story of this man:
Failed in business - Age 22
Ran for legislature (defeated) - Age 23
Again failed in business - Age 24
Elected to legislature - Age 25

Sweetheart died - Age 26
Had a nervous breakdown - Age 27
Defeated for Speaker - Age 29
Defeated for Elector - Age 31
Defeated for Congress - Age 34
Elected to Congress - Age 37
Defeated for Congress - Age 39
Defeated for Senate - Age 46
Defeated for Vice President - Age 47
Defeated for Senate - Age 49
Elected President of the United States - Age 51

The man, of course, was Abraham Lincoln and he is a testament that success is failure turned inside out. It is critical to understand that, as you attempt greatness, you will risk failure. That's a byproduct of achievement. However, failure is not your enemy. Complacency and fear are. For you cannot fail if you do not try. But if you do not try, then by default you have already failed. "My great concern," said Lincoln, "is not whether you have failed, but whether you are content with your failure."

HOW YOUR CUSTOMERS WANT TO BUY THEIR NEW HOMES/HOMESITES

Curious about what customers expect from a salesperson? Based upon my personal survey's, this is what they said. How do you rate?

♦ **"Listen to me."**

Understand that listening is the first commandment of sales because listening is learning. Listening establishes the prospects' needs and helps you ferret out their reasons for wanting a new home. Are they looking for security? Status? Are they moving up in the world or scaling down? What is their passion? From their viewpoint, what is motivating them?

♦ **"Give me a good reason why your neighborhood and home is perfect for me."**

If you have questioned skillfully and listened carefully, you will have an understanding of how to present the benefits (hot buttons) that match each customer's unique set of circumstances.

♦ **"Show me I am not a pioneer.** Tell me how someone similar to me succeeded by owning a home/homesite in this or a similar community."

Few buyers want to feel as though they are the first or the only, so restore your customers' confidence by confirming their decisions to purchase. Use third party testimonials, show them a published article and demonstrate that people just like them are happy with their decisions.

♦ **"Tell me how you will serve me after you help me become an owner."**

Some people inherently don't trust salespeople because previously they have been sold nothing but empty promises. Express to them the commitment to customer satisfaction that is shared by you and your company.

♦ **"Make sure you convey to me that the price is fair."**

Buyers want reassurance that the price they are paying is the absolute best value, as they perceive it. Remember, it is a misconception that customers are only concerned with the lowest price. Equally if not more important is your timely delivery, consistent follow up, faithful follow through, and commitment to your customer's best interest.

♦ **"Don't argue with me.** Even if I am wrong, I don't want to be told so."

Keep in mind the adage: A man convinced against his will is of the same opinion still.

♦ **"Show me the best way to pay."**

Of the six top fears for acquiring real estate, two of them center on financial concerns. Your customers need information and help in understanding financial alternatives.

♦ **"Give me a choice.** Let me decide, but make consultative recommendations. Don't confuse me. The more complicated it is, the less likely I am to buy. I may be nervous and need you to assure my decision with facts that help me feel confident."

♦ **"Deliver to me what you sold me.** I've just given you my hard-earned money (security) and, in essence, have traded my money for your promises. If I give you my money and you disappoint me, I may never do business with you again or give you referrals."

♦ **"Follow up with me in the manner in which I prefer to communicate."**

Customers are beginning to shop differently. They are using the Internet to begin and end their buying processes. If that's how they communicate, don't waste their time contacting them with antiquated methods of follow up.

Bottom line: Customers don't take the time to consciously critique your sales process. They just say no. And that's a word you want to avoid.

DEFINING SUCCESS

What is your definition of success? A thousand people will offer a thousand and one different answers. Is it fame, money, spirituality, good health, the pursuit of personal happiness? Or perhaps none of those. Author and motivational speaker Earl Nightingale expressed it this way: Success is the progressive realization of a worthwhile goal.

You may be rushing to achieve, but before you begin the journey toward success, take time to define it. Since our lives are ongoing realities, true success must be part of the journey. And only you can describe what a successful life means to you.

To do that, start now by choosing specific goals and their completion dates. Allow yourself enough time to grow and develop before reaching them. Control your destiny instead of having it control you and success will end up being your constant companion. Become a success on your own terms. Think deeply about what it means to you and then consistently act on your conclusions and convictions. Nothing will give you more satisfaction than being the architect of your own goals as you navigate life's journey.

DON'T TAKE IT PERSONALLY

You have probably heard the story of the Wright Brothers. Both were bicycle mechanics who were unknown and lacking a formal education. Although they weren't leaders in aviation, they still managed to pioneer man's first motorized flight on December 17, 1903.

But do you know the story of Samuel P. Langley? He was a professor of mathematics and astronomy, and a Director of the Smithsonian Institution. Langley was also a scientist and inventor who, in the mid to late 1890's, actively performed experiments with large unmanned airplane models, gaining notable recognition for his accomplishments.

Because he was at the forefront of aviation, the U.S. War Department gave him $50,000 (an astronomical amount of money for that time) and commissioned him to design and build an airplane that would send mankind skyward.

By 1901, he had successfully tested and created history's first heavier-than-air aircraft. Then, on October 8, 1903, on a modified houseboat in front of journalists and spectators, Langley (with the aid of pilot Charles Manley) attempted to fly his plane, The Great Aerodrome.

When the launch was attempted, however, the biplane was flung into sixteen feet of water only 50 feet from the boat. Criticism from skeptics and cynics was brutal as evidenced by this report in the New York Times:

"The ridiculous fiasco, which attended the attempt at aerial navigation in the Langley flying machine, was not unexpected. No doubt the problem has its attractions for those it interests, but to ordinary men, it would seem as if the effort might be employed more profitably."

At first, Langley remained undaunted. Eight weeks later in early December he and his pilot again prepared to make history with their second flight. Yet, once again, disaster struck and this time the pilot nearly died.

As before the cynics and skeptics fiercely attacked the Great Aerodrome, calling it "Langley's Folly," and accused him of wasting government funds.

Langley succumbed to his critics and abandoned his project with the heavy-hearted speech, "I have brought to close the portion of work which seemed to be specifically mine—the demonstration of the practicality of mechanical flight. For the next stage, which is the commercial and practical development of the idea, it is probable that the world may look to others."

Instead of throwing his hat in the ring, Langley threw in the towel. He abandoned his pursuit of flight and walked away from his decade-long pursuit. Only a few days later, Orville and Wilbur Wright—uneducated, unknown and unfunded—flew their aircraft from the sand dunes of Kitty Hawk, North Carolina.

Let me offer my perspective of Langley and the Wright Brothers because what happened to them is what occurs in the lives of many people today. Too many allow failure and setbacks to get the best of them, while a few accept life's challenges as lessons and allow their setbacks to propel them toward the achievement of their goals.

In retrospect, it would seem that Samuel Langley had an almost unfair advantage over the Wright Brothers; money, education, reputation and supporters. Yet, I suggest it was the Wright Brothers who had the unfair advantage over Langley.

Samuel Langley had more than his share of cynics and skeptics surrounding his project. As painful as failure can be, it's magnified when others add their ridicule. This would cause him, and anyone else, to emotionalize and personalize their shortcomings. For many, the pain of failure leads to the fear of failure.

Because the Wright Brothers were unknown, they had no cynics or skeptics to criticize their work. The advantage they had over Langley was that, when they experienced setbacks, their thoughts were not on personalized failure but on focusing on the lessons of their failures.

Therefore, the first and most important step in overcoming failure (setbacks, obstacles and challenges) is to understand that failure is an event and not a person. It is something that happens to you that can be demoralizing as well as educational, but it is not YOU. To put it simply, failing to achieve does not make you a failure.

If you really want to accomplish your dreams, you must get into the marketplace, take calculated risks and be willing to experience failure. Soccer player Kyle Rote, Jr. noted, "There are many ways to win, but only one way to lose and that is to fail and not look beyond the failure."

Big shots are little shots who kept right on shooting.

~ Zig Ziglar

There are only three things to know about how to get what you want. One, decide what you want. Two, decide what you are willing to give up to get it. And three, go for it.

~ H.L. Hunt

TAKE A LESSON
FROM PROCTOR &
GAMBLE

The message appeared in my e-mail from a young builder who had worked in his father's home-building company from the time he was a teenager. Now, in his mid-thirties, he has started his own business. His message read: "We need help. We built a model home, a glorious one for the parade of homes that received 95 percent approval on exit polls. Yet, it hasn't sold and the interest meter is ticking. Our advertising isn't working. We're not salespeople; we are builders. What do we do?"

His situation isn't unusual. For the most part, builders and developers have a habit of entering the marketplace with what is known as the "Field of Dreams" mentality—if we build it they will come (and buy). Usually, they say, they followed their "sixth sense," a perception or "their gut feeling" in building what they perceived the market needs.

The Four P's

Construction, like sales, is a science and with any science gut feelings and hunches do not play a role when entering the marketplace. A good business plan should be developed with a solid strategy and an understanding that selling and marketing new homes consists of four components. Labeled the Four P's, they were popularized by Proctor & Gamble and utilized by industry giants such as General Electric and Microsoft. The Four P's are effective because they break the sales and marketing process into four parts: Place, Product, Price & Promotion.

Place: If you have been in real estate or community sales for any length of time, you have probably learned the adage: The three keys to real estate, are location, location, location. Well, it's absolutely true.

The successful builder/developer understands that people don't just live in homes. They live in a particular area, within the confines of a neighborhood in which the homes are located. Location is the factor that separates one neighborhood from another. Any builder/developer can, for the most part, construct homes at approximately the same cost per square foot, provided comparable materials are used. But the one single factor that changes the perception of value is where one home is located over another.

Product: Who is your competition? It is either other builders, or, in the case of an established neighborhood, the competition may be the resale market. In either case, if you cannot enter or establish a market with a perceived value that surpasses your competition, then consider "creative abandonment."

When evaluating the types of housing designs and floor plans, study the area's past 12 to 24 month sale's history. If a distinct market-share has been established with three-bedroom, 2.5 bath homes, then do not attempt to reinvent the wheel. Enter the marketplace with a proven design and simply add enhancements such as vaulted ceilings, spa baths, walk-in closets or a better use of square footage. Then, you are sure to gain your fair percentage of market share.

Price: Again, gut feelings and hunches play no role in determining the price point when you enter the marketplace. Price cannot ultimately be determined by your desire for a certain profit margin, but rather by what the consumer has paid in the past.

Price is easily determined by comparable values, which can be accessed through MLS. To disregard historical pricing data and produce a product at prices that are not proven in the marketplace is writing your own invitation to disaster.

Promotion: Contrary to popular belief, promotion is not limited to just a good "sales process." To reach a target audience, you must effectively plan and budget. My personal belief is that your marketing, merchandising and products should be so good that they could almost make you, as a salesperson, obsolete.

Rethinking the Sale's Process:

With housing products looking more like commodities and with stiffer competition, today's great salespeople have developed a new mindset. They recognize that success no longer depends on communicating the value of the offering, but instead rests on the salesperson's ability to "create value" for customers.

Builders and developers who delude themselves into believing that selling is easy and strictly a function of foot-traffic (and then transfer that concept to their sale's team), will be beat like a drum in the marketplace.

It is important to grasp this truth: a sale's process is a series of actions and systems directed toward the end result, which is causing a sale on purpose.

In most cases, failure in the marketplace is the result of poor planning. The Four P's—Place, Product, Price and Promotion—are like a four-legged stool. If each is not weighted proportionately and then backed with a proven sale's process, the stool will wobble and become unbalanced. If the four areas are not balanced, you may see your sales topple just like a lopsided stool.

It's the job that's never started that takes longest to finish.

~ J.R.R. Tolkien

28½ DARN GOOD REASONS NOT TO MAKE THE SALE

G reat salespeople are always prepared whenever they are faced with quarterly performance evaluations. That's why they are never caught without a grab bag of sound excuses for not making enough sales when confronted by their sale's manager. Here are a few excuses you can use to encourage nods of agreement and may even elicit a word or two of sympathy.

Sale's Manager: So, I notice your sales are down this month. What happened?

Your response: (Choose one) ☺

1. The construction schedule for amenities was not met. How can I sell something my customers can't see?

2. You made me role-play in front of a group. It unnerved me for the whole month.

3. My people always come in when we have sale's meetings so I miss them.

4. I haven't had my morning coffee and can't think right now.

5. I took your advice and it didn't work.

6. I didn't take your advice and should have.

7. My horoscope predictions said to take it easy this month.

8. My best appointments are always scheduled during sale's training.

9. How can I make new sales when I'm focused on holding my deals together?

10. Walk-in traffic is off.

11. I couldn't get my mind off the declining economy. People just don't have money to spend right now.

12. Hey, aren't I entitled to a social life?

13. Weather or other natural events I have no control over have impacted the market and affected my sale's totals.

14. Walk-in traffic shows up during the most inconvenient times, usually when I'm trying to catch-up on my follow-up. I can't do everything.

15. It's not easy being me. I have a lot of emotional baggage to deal with, you know.

16. I've been doing this for 10-years and have never had to use a computer or the Internet to make a sale.

17. You expect me to memorize a script? I don't think so.

18. The brochures are outdated.

19. My spouse/significant other just won't leave me alone so I'm having trouble concentrating.

20. There's so much pressure knowing this is the month the professional shopper is doing on-site evaluations.

21. There was a full moon the previous night and I didn't sleep well.

22. My allergies are killing me. I'm not as productive as I normally am.

23. I'm overwhelmed with work. I need an assistant.

24. Once this (whatever) is behind me, I'll be able to focus.

25. We need to negotiate prices.

26. The orange barrels around the entryway construction have confused my customers and they can't find me.

27. Our registration policy is bad. Other salespeople keep stealing my customers.

28. The co-broke community just doesn't cooperate.

28½. Space debris fell into the parking lot and I've been busy helping NASA.

Of course, there are many more time-tested excuses that can be used, abused and embellished. So be creative. But be careful. Especially if you begin repeating the excuse, "My sales are down because my competitor is taking all my clients."

That one just might be true.

HOW TO MAKE YOUR PROSPECT CONFIDENT ENOUGH TO BUY

Your prospects will not own if they lack confidence in you, your neighborhood or your homes. You must use sale's tools, stories and examples in a way that allows your prospects to relate ownership of your product to their unique set of circumstances.

Besides the basics—be on time, be enthusiastic and look professional—here are methods you can employ to instill confidence:

♦ *Be completely prepared.* A fumbling, excuse-making salesperson builds zero confidence.

♦ *Have something in writing.* An article about your company or product from a national news source elevates your credibility.

♦ *Emphasize customer satisfaction and service after the sale.* Today's buyer wants to be certain you will not sell and skidoodle.

♦ *Sell to serve—not for commission.* New home and neighborhood selling is not something you do to a person, but something you do for them. Prospects can sense a greedy salesperson.

♦ *Ask the right questions.* Avoid bombarding the prospect with information overload. Zig Ziglar advises, "People don't care how much you know. They first want to know how much you care." The most important link to the sale's process is to ask the right questions.

♦ *Organize customer testimonials.* Obtain letters that cover various aspects of your business—quality, service, on-time delivery. Be sure your letters answer the buyer's objections. Also, on high quality letterhead, print a list of satisfied customers.

♦ *Tell third-party stories of how you helped another customer in a similar situation.* Your prospects do not want to feel as if they are pioneers.

They want assurance others "just like them" acquired a home or homesite for the same reasons.

♦ *Build a meaningful referral business.* Results depend on relationships. Remember that you earn referrals by excelling in service.

Most of us as individuals act as though we think the future is something that happens to us, rather than something we create everyday. Many people explain their current activities in terms of where they have been rather than in terms of where they are going. Because it's over, the past is unmanageable. Because it has not happened, the future is manageable.

~ Herbert Shepard

SALE'S MEETINGS THAT GUARANTEE RESULTS

Meetings are "management in action," and are opportunities for people to gather in groups to solve problems, make decisions, share information and exchange views and opinions.

However, meetings are like advertising. It is estimated that 50 percent of all the dollars spent on advertising is wasted, but no one is certain which 50 percent it is so they don't know what to eliminate. In meetings, it is also estimated that 50 percent of the time is wasted, but no one is quite certain which is the unnecessary half to eliminate.

As a New Home and Neighborhood Sales Manager, the way you conduct a meeting and your performance in a meeting are major factors comprising a successful career. In a meeting you are observed by both supervisors and subordinates. You can beam—or you can bomb—but you cannot hide.

A MEETING IS AN INVESTMENT

There is a cost associated with each meeting; therefore, there must be a return (profit) in excess of the cost. To determine the cost, multiply the average profit of just one home or homesite sale that could occur during your sales meeting. Also, take into account the average commission and wages of the participants, times the number of hours of the meeting.

The cost of a meeting is never taken into account, yet you will find this one simple exercise reveals a huge expenditure that normally equates to thousands of dollars an hour. Bottom line: You are in business to create a profit and there is no justifiable reason to be in business without profiting. Therefore, if you discover your sale's meeting is an expenditure that equals thousands of dollars per hour, then the return on your investment must be greater than the cost of the meeting.

Why do most salespeople justifiably dislike sales meetings?

1. The meeting has no written agenda.

2. The meeting is run by someone who is uncomfortable with, or who cannot facilitate, a meeting.

3. Most meetings are glorified policy sessions and the topics center around forms, paperwork and trivial non-sales-related topics that take twice as long as they should to discuss and will probably change next week.

4. Meetings do not have enough "real world" selling lessons.

5. Most meetings start and end late, allowing latecomers to penalize the prompt attendees.

6. Some salespeople people think they know everything and should be out selling and earning a profit instead of wasting time in a meeting.

So what is the solution? How do you design and conduct a great sale's meeting every time? It's simple: plan and prepare. Set an agenda and stick to it. Make it fun, be productive and include participation by everyone. Here are some tips:

♦ Always have a written agenda. The biggest mistake is to think the only one who needs an agenda is you. Organize your topics in order of importance and distribute the agenda 24 to 48 hours in advance so participants can be prepared.

♦ Avoid the Demotivators. The most unsuccessful meetings do things like going over paperwork, company policies, handling personal disputes and verbally re-enforcing what's wrong. Try this: Have an instruction sheet for the new policy and/or forms and deliver it by e-mail. Include specific instructions in your e-mail and always give the reason(s) why this new policy or form is necessary. Conclude your e-mail by stating: Questions and concerns about the policy or form are to be directed to me.

♦ Have your meeting early in the morning. Include healthier foods such as bagels, fresh fruit and juice, water and plenty of hot coffee prepared in advance. Avoid the pastries and soft drinks. They deplete energy and actually cause a lack of participation.

♦ Like a good razor: Start sharp, end sharp, be sharp. Fine the late ones or simply shut the door. Regardless, START ON TIME, END ON TIME and MOTIVATE OTHERS TO FOLLOW YOUR LEAD.

◆ Stress the positive. Support your people in public, especially among their peers and in front of management. If you have a negative participant or a negative comment to make, be sure to say it to him or her privately.

◆ Use the meeting as a weekly training session. Remember your return on investment. The goal is to motivate, teach and learn. The training can be A) led by the manager B) provided by experts C) led by individual salespeople or D) enhanced by role-playing and/or videotapes and books.

◆ Use the meeting to update the staff's product knowledge. Let construction and/or land planning experts from other departments within your company keep the team abreast of new materials and processes, as well as sharpen the team's construction knowledge.

◆ Reward positive behaviors from the previous week. Present awards and share plenty of success stories. This helps people feel better when they leave the meeting than when they arrived and they'll anticipate the next one.

◆ Relate expectations of the upcoming week. Have each salesperson verbally affirm what they will accomplish and have each manager affirm how they will assist the salesperson in the accomplishment of the goal.

◆ End on a high note. Include two to three minutes of a motivational highlight, a success story of a team member, a quote, a video clip or an inspirational reading. Give the team something that causes them to walk through the wall rather than leave through the door.

Meetings should help salespeople people stay focused on the result—making the sale. In the face of your day-to-day responsibilities, your meetings are the only "group opportunity" to make a substantial difference. Those attending are exchanging something very valuable and irreplaceable—their time—in order to be there. So don't disappoint them.

FRIENDLY COMPETITION? YEAH, RIGHT!

How do you feel about your competition? You may say, "I have a great relationship with my competitors." But think about it. Given the choice of having you in business or out of business, your competitors would probably give you directions to the unemployment office before they'd direct you to a potential sale.

Friendly competition—an oxymoron—two words that contradict each other like "act naturally, large shrimp, alone together, dress pants and pretty ugly." It would be nice if the words "friendly competition" were synonymous ... if all salespeople took turns ... played fair ... looked out for each other. If you went to work one day and your closest competitor said, "Hey, look I got the last sale for my builder. It's only fair that the next one is yours, so here's a lead to follow up."

For those of you who are convinced that there's plenty of room for everyone, consider this: Suppose there was space for only one neighborhood in your market and a new developer was ready to set up business in your backyard. Would you still feel there's plenty of room if your paycheck were suddenly divided by two?

A little competition can keep you on your toes while too much can knock you off your feet. As with all areas of life, there's a healthy balance. Find it. And, since you will have competition, learn to deal with it and maximize its benefits. Here are some suggestions.

What's the reality about your competition?

♦ Some competitors are truly good.

♦ Some will cooperate.

♦ Some are highly ethical.

♦ Some will trade business with you.

♦ Some will help you.

♦ But most of your competitors are the opposite of "friendly." Although they aren't hostile, they also aren't eager to share profits and prospects. They will probably be uncooperative, unmotivated and disinterested in helping you succeed. Internally, they are probably wishing you would find another profession or at least move outside their market territory.

So, how should you approach them?

♦ Competition should not establish battlegrounds. Don't focus on the fight. Instead, learn all you can, be prepared and do your best.

♦ Shop them regularly. Know how they sell and how customers perceive the benefits of doing business with them.

♦ Identify their shortcomings.

♦ Identify their strengths and then strengthen your shortcomings.

♦ Get every piece of their information, brochures, prices, etc. that you can and review it.

♦ Know where they stand in the marketplace. What's their reputation?

How should you react when going toe-to-toe against the competition with a customer?

♦ Never say anything bad about them, even if they criticize you in front of the prospect.

Remember, "When you dig dirt, you are bound to lose ground." Maintain your ethics and integrity—even if it means biting your tongue until it bleeds.

♦ Show them respect.

♦ Ask clients a three-part question: Mr. & Mrs. Prospect, I am sure you would agree a new home/homesite is a large investment, wouldn't you? Specifically, what would cause you to make such a significant investment with A.B.C. Builders? Is there some particular reason you prefer doing business with them?

♦ Show them how you differ; how your benefits are superior.

♦ Stress your strengths.

♦ Share a testimonial (third party endorsement) of a customer who was in a similar situation and decided to do business with you. "My other customers thought the same thing as you until they discovered ..."

♦ Follow-up ... regardless. In the event you do not conclude the sale on the first visit, remember that customers are fickle and will often sacrifice price and square footage for a trusting relationship.

◆ In the event you do not capture the sale, ask yourself: What have I learned and what can I do to safeguard against a similar situation in the future? Do I need to make changes in my presentation? My appearance? My approach? My communication skills?

*All of our dreams can come true – if
we have the courage to pursue them.*

~ Walt Disney

RAISING THE BAR

Today, you are in a unique position to accumulate and enjoy all the rewards that new community/new home sales will offer in the future.

To do this, however, you must begin a journey—one that will increase your sales, improve your income and involve you in merging your dreams with reality.

The journey is one of change. In order to experience an improvement of any kind, you must be willing to do something different. Specifically, you must be willing to make certain changes in your life.

Think about your own personal performance. How do you rate your current skills compared to

10 years ago? How about five years ago? One year ago?

If you are not making significant efforts to continually improve (change), you're falling behind. Why? Because your competition is continually raising the bar ... advancing ... redefining the playing field. Want proof?

In 1972 Mark Spitz literally dominated the Olympic swimming competition with an unprecedented seven gold medals. In 1996, Spitz would not have made the team with his then record-breaking times.

At the 1980 Olympic Games, Eric Heiden won five gold medals in speed skating. By the 1998 Olympics, his fastest gold-medal time would have put him in 40th place!

In 1994 Dan Jansen blew away the 1,000-meter competition. Yet, four years later, his times would have put him in 19th place.

Professional golfers Jack Nicholas and Arnold Palmer, both high achievers in their first 100 professional starts, respectively dominated the record books. By the time Tiger Woods completed his first 100 professional starts he had walked all over both Jack's and Arnie's personal best.

These examples remind us that, in our profession as well as in sports, strategies we employed last year may be outdated or obsolete today. Plus there's always someone waiting in the wings to surpass us. As the expression goes, "when you make your mark in the world, look out for guys with erasers."

Don't make the mistake of believing that there is nothing new to learn, or you already know it all. Personal development, commitment to excellence and being the best in your field is akin to running a race without a finish line. There is no end. But that is good. Because it challenges us to work to become ... not to acquire.

Our goals can only be reached through a vehicle of a plan, in which we must fervently believe, and upon which we must vigorously act. There is no other route to success.

~ Stephen A Brennen

INDEX

A great percentage of Myers' work is with organizations just like yours. Undoubtedly, the keys to his outstanding success are his abilities to present dynamic, customized programs, based on the unique need of the company and its people. His presentations are high energy, motivational and in all cases produce bottom-line results.

To increase your organization's profits, as well as enrich, enlighten and entertain, contact:

Myers Barnes Associates, Inc.
Post Office Box 50
Kitty Hawk, North Carolina 27949
Phone: 252-261-7611
Fax: 252-261-7615
E-mail: sellmore@myersbarnes.com
Or, visit our web site at
www.myersbarnes.com